ASHES AND THE PHŒNIX

MEDITATIONS FOR THE SEASON OF LENT

The collects (prayers) for the weeks of Lent and for the days of Holy Week can be found in *The Book of Common Prayer*.

Forward
Movement

ASHES AND THE PHŒNIX

MEDITATIONS FOR THE SEASON OF LENT

Poetry by Len Freeman

with Cynthia Cannon, Mary W. Cox, Jason Leo,
Teresa Pasquale Mateus, C. K. Robertson,
Glenice Robinson-Como, and Porter Taylor

Woodcuts by Jason Sierra

Contents

A Note to Readers

The meditations, poems, and artwork in *Ashes and the Phoenix: Meditations for the Season of Lent* offer many paths for you to walk with Jesus toward Jerusalem. The meditations from noted authors and faithful pilgrims may speak to your heart. The poetry may stir you, and the original artwork move you. Or perhaps you will connect most strongly with the collects. It may be tempting to focus on only one component of this book. But as is a custom during Lent, we encourage you not to give into temptation. See and experience this book as a companion—a kind of field guide through the wilderness and wildness of the season.

Engage *Ashes and the Phoenix* in different ways: the collects from *The Book of Common Prayer* and related woodcuts inspired by the gospels; the daily meditations; the original poems for each day. We left blank space around the poems and throughout the book, as well as a few pages at the end so that, if inspired, you can write your own travel log, all season long. We love the idea of you composing poems or collects in the margins, making notes about the meditations, captioning the artwork as you make your pilgrimage from Ash Wednesday to Easter Sunday.

This is your book—use it in any and every way that meets your spiritual needs and goals. Should you desire to write a collect, the formula is pretty simple: address God by whatever name works best for you, follow it with an attribute of God that you particularly want to focus your prayer around, and proceed to the petition or praise aspect of your prayer. Then end with an expression of thanksgiving. In the introduction, poet Len Freeman offers helpful suggestions to encourage writing poetry. And we commend to you the personal and theologically insightful meditations as models for writing your own responses.

God bless you on your journey through a holy Lent.

RACHEL JONES, EDITOR

A Word of Introduction

The poem-prayers in this book came over the course of one Lenten season as expressions of my own soul's journey. But they also came as words back to me. I believe that the poetic voice is one of the ways God speaks to us from the inside to say, "Hello there!" and guide us on the way.

One of the hopes of this book is that you might be encouraged to write your own poetry or engage in some other creative expression as part of your own conversation with God during this Lenten season.

Writing poetry is not about meeting some particular academic form or standard. Crafting a poem is about letting your heart get out ahead of your head and allowing the words to flow, trusting that your "down deep" has something to tell you, something to say. The connection to that deep self (that silly self, that playful self) comes from the heart of God, and this is why what comes out of our soul's deep well is sometimes a word of God, from God.

Prayer is a way of communicating with God, involving both parties sending and receiving all sorts of information. We focus a lot on the part where we send information to God, working on perfecting our messages. The sending part of prayer often comes down to some variation of help, thank you, or oops. Most of us need some work on tuning into the receiving part— the part where we listen to and receive the word of God.

Poetry turns out to be one of those avenues where sending and receiving can come together. We can let our hearts and minds flow out in words and then step back to see what God has to say to us.

One of the things that helped me send and receive in the poetry of prayer was a commitment I made several years ago to take a walk and to write a poem every day. The nice thing about writing a new poem every day is that I know I'm not trying to write grand epics like *Evangeline* or *Thanatopsis*. Writing every day frees me up to not have to be perfect. I just write one poem. One. And I don't sweat it. I move on. Or let it be. My suspicion is that this method can work for most people, and I encourage you to try it as you move through Lent with Jesus and this book as your companions.

What form to follow? If you can rhyme, (*I think that I shall never see a thing as lovely as a tree*) fine. But poems are not obliged to rhyme. Part of writing poetry is letting the words come to you without forcing them into a particular set form. Try writing something simple—a thought that comes out in three or four short lines. Play with your verse by having the final line be just one word. Or having each line be shorter than the last or capitalize first lines, or not—just do something to push the words around on the page and to push your brain to see something new in the words. See what naturally comes. And don't worry if the poems are long or short, or all the same or each one different. These are yours, and they are just what they need to be.

Finding a time and place to help you feel encouraged and inspired to write are important to your exercise. The green chair in our bedroom is a natural place for me to sit with my laptop at the end of a day to do my writing. The advantage to end-of-day writing is that I have plenty of images, phrases, and moments from the day for inspiration.

Writing just a single word, just putting pen to paper. Eking out a phrase or describing an image—that's how I usually start. C.S. Lewis's entire *Chronicles of Narnia* came out of an image he had in his head of a lamppost in a patch of woods. Everyday life can provide a lot of grist for the mill. You may also find it helpful to have a source to bounce your poems off each day. For the poem-prayers in this book I used the collects for Lent, the readings for the saints' days, and the Great Litany, all of which can be found in *The Book of Common Prayer*. You could also use your Facebook feed or the collection of fortunes from your favorite Chinese restaurant—something to inspire or encourage you.

Whatever your nudge is, wherever your writing place is, whatever time of day you choose to do it, go with it. Stay with it. See where it takes you. And then, step back and see what God has had to say back to you in the doing.

Blessings,

Len Freeman

THE WEEK OF ASH WEDNESDAY

Worthily Lamenting
Our Sins

Almighty and everlasting God, you hate nothing you have made and forgive the sins of all who are penitent: Create and make in us new and contrite hearts, that we, worthily lamenting our sins and acknowledging our wretchedness, may obtain of you, the God of all mercy, perfect remission and forgiveness; through Jesus Christ our Lord, who lives and reigns with you and the Holy Spirit, one God, for ever and ever. Amen.

Ash Wednesday

"Ashes! Ashes! We all fall down!" For centuries, children have sung variations of the song "Ring Around the Roses." There is no certain history behind this macabre childhood song, and the line "Ashes, ashes, we all fall down" seems strange and abrupt for a nursery rhyme. While we may not have a clear explanation of the origin or meaning of the lyrics, we know that in the biblical context, ashes represent sorrow and repentance. Ashes serve as a sign that we are formed from dust, and it is to dust that we are most assuredly going.

Ash Wednesday marks the beginning of Lent, reminding us of our mortality and humanity. During this season, we are called to develop spiritual disciplines, recognize our wrongdoings, and accept that in the midst of this life, we fall down.

Our fallings and failings are not the totality of our story, nor do they signal the end of God's loving presence and providential activity in our lives. It is in the fallen, cratered-out spaces of our lives that we are most deeply reminded of a loving God who always offers us a way out of the ashes and into new life. In these collapsed voids, we are invited to find strength in weakness and hope in despair. Within the ashes, God's love steadfastly abides, transforming our broken lives into overflowing vessels of service—mended and made whole. On this Ash Wednesday, may we release the sins of the past to unveil our deepest fears, our failings, and the ways we fall down. May we remember God is mighty, able to exchange our ashes for crowns of beauty, the oil of joy for our mourning, and garments of praise for our despair.

—GLENICE ROBINSON-COMO

❧

Ashes speak to me
of what matters and
what does not.

Remind me of the heart
of my heart and that I
and the ones I love

are more than what
will dribble into the
ground.

May I be thankful
that I await not just
the ashes

but the Phoenix.

Thursday after
Ash Wednesday

Lent is a season of fresh starts and new beginnings. As the liturgy for Ash Wednesday says, Lent is a season for "self-examination and repentance," for "prayer, fasting, and self-denial." All this is right and good. The danger is that we fall into a trap of thinking that Lent (and life) is all about us, about what we do. Lent can become another New Year's, colored by making resolutions about what we will give up and what we will take on. Self-examination and self-discipline are good things, but we will miss something very important if we don't move beyond ourselves and our efforts.

It is God who directs us with gracious favor. It is God who furthers us with continual help. And it is God, who out of the deep well of divine mercy, makes everlasting, abundant life a reality. Saint Paul's letter to the Christians living in Philippi reminds us that the One who began a good work in us will indeed bring that work to completion. It is not up to us to finish this work all by ourselves, and it never has been.

This is why Lent is a gift. If everything is up to us all the time, life can become exhausting. The good news of Lent is that the One who knows us—our stories, our failures, our burdens—is with us. So we can dare to be honest with ourselves, because God already knows all of it. The Lenten disciplines we set for ourselves are right and good. But let us never fool ourselves into thinking that we are our own saviors. There is already one who claims that title. And that merciful Savior is not done with us yet.

—C. K. ROBERTSON

⤫

Failures, a part of our stories
whose burden we bear, by
whose grace we have
grown.

I give thanks to you Lord
for these moments, these graces,
that touched down in my life
along the way

to save me.

Friday after
Ash Wednesday

Jesus knows we carry with us a burden of hurt too heavy to bear—beyond what we are called to carry by life or circumstance. The gravity of this unbearable burden keeps us from the truest and holiest part of ourselves. We embody an emotional masochism that cuts us to the core of our heart and our spirit—and the burden is too heavy to carry.

In this season of lament, we hold space, grief, the sacredness of our pain, and the wounds we carry (inflicted on us, inflicted on others, inflicted on ourselves). These tight and tender feelings are all real and true, and they deserve to be observed by our sitting in prayer and sacred silence, out of reverence and respect for their existence.

This contemplation and concentration seems to stir something in us—calling us to give up the ghosts of our unforgotten sins, because even the unforgotten is still forgiven. We are forgiven in the highest court, where no one is sentenced to death, and restored to the holy place where Jesus offers us emancipation from our pain. We are asked in this season to move through our pain, feel the immeasurable weight of what we carry, and then let it go. The burden of our pain is too heavy, and there is a lighter one awaiting us—a mantle that holds the message of sacred calling in its folds. We must give up the ghosts to live into our present and be the fullness of who we are called to be, for this time, and this place, and this beautiful, broken world.

—TERESA PASQUALE MATEUS

❧

Let me this day be
open to what I can
let go of and what
needs to be
taken up.

Saturday after
Ash Wednesday

In his novel, *The Natural*, Bernard Malamud writes, "We have two lives... the life we learn with and the life we live after that. Suffering is what brings us toward happiness." American culture presupposes that the goal of life is to be immune from suffering. If we own enough or obtain enough illusions of power and self-sufficiency, we can somehow escape our limitations and our sinfulness. Life has a way of reminding us that we are not in control. We end up admitting, "I've fallen, and I can't get up," over and over again, because the truth is we cannot manage our lives. We can only endeavor to live our lives faithfully. Crying out, "I've fallen," is a doorway to remembering God.

The life we learn with is the knowledge of our sinfulness, discovering over and over again the smallness of our personal agendas. We lament our sins, not because we despise ourselves, but because we know that without God, we cannot get up.

The lives we live after learning our limits and admitting the narrowness of our visions begin with turning to God and asking, "Please, Lord...help me up." We begin lives of discipleship—which are always lives of falling down and asking for help. Jesus can do little with the Pharisees or anyone filled with self-righteousness who cannot (or will not) lament their sins and ask for God's help. But Jesus always turns to those who have no illusions about their abilities, who are humble, who cry out to him, who reach out their hands to him in love and hope. They know they have no power to raise themselves up or to make their lives work. Jesus always hears us when we cry out: "Help me up."

—PORTER TAYLOR

❧

I've fallen and I
can't get up...

I've fallen and I
can't get up...

I've fallen and I
can't get up.

Please, Lord...
help me up.

THE FIRST WEEK IN LENT

Mighty To Save

Almighty God, whose blessed Son was led by the Spirit to be tempted by Satan: Come quickly to help us who are assaulted by many temptations; and as you know the weaknesses of each of us, let each one find you mighty to save; through Jesus Christ your Son our Lord, who lives and reigns with you and the Holy Spirit, one God, now and for ever. Amen.

SUNDAY, LENT I

During Lent, Jesus invites us to revisit the denial and betrayal and unhealed traumas in our own lives and ask for healing. How can we walk through our memories and guilt again? What is the point? We like to tell ourselves that the greatest losses in our lives will happen as we age—hearing, eyesight, mobility. For some though, the harshest betrayals happened when we were children. The people who should have loved us most in the world all too often lashed out from their own pain, smashing our small dreams. They cut us with their words; some of them may have physically injured us.

Suffer the little children to come to me. Jesus knows how hard it is for a child to grow up and recover from these early, chronic injuries. Grief is like a Mobius Strip—it cannot be oriented but merely spirals and fluctuates. Lent is the season to look deeply at our own grief and bring it to Jesus. Like Jesus, we know betrayal is the deepest cut—a bitter cup to drink. But we are called to sit with our own injuries and avoid the temptation to look away, for it is only through accepting the truth that we can begin to heal. How effortlessly and often have we been betrayed and injured? We want to move on but we must not. We must not domesticate our heartbreaking losses. We dare not tame them nor welcome them to stay.

—CYNTHIA CANNON

the sun shines on
my frozen world
the ice melting
through.

may it be so
with my heart.

MONDAY, LENT I

On the night the Cuban Missile Crisis began, I was planning to write a musical.

I listened as President John F. Kennedy delivered the grim news of Soviet ships heading toward Cuba with a cargo of nuclear missiles. An American naval blockade had been deployed to turn them back to their own shores.

I was terrified by the news and stunned—but an hour after the press conference, I was sitting in my English professor's living room, meeting with faculty members to talk about writing a musical, an allegory of education and life. They had approached my English professor about writing the book and lyrics, and she offered my hand to help, since I wrote (and still write) verse.

That night we briefly acknowledged that this missile crisis business sounded pretty bad—but we moved on to our project. The faculty members outlined their concept, and I took notes and scribbled ideas for songs. I don't recall that we prayed together, pondering and puzzling over this troubling news. But it felt like our whole conversation that evening was a prayer, bidding God to make sure that everything good and beautiful in our lives would continue.

A few days later, I wrote to my parents that it might seem ridiculous under the shadow of nuclear war to make plans to write a musical. I told them, "I believe that any act of creativity is an act against destruction." I think my 20-year-old self got that right.

We never finished our musical, but on that terrifying night, our creative collaboration was an act of trust in the creating God who is "mighty to save."

—MARY W. COX

❧

dark night black
yet calm. like the
inside of a soul
that has not yet
seen the light
but knows

that it is
coming.

thank you, Lord
for the impulse
of creation.

TUESDAY, LENT I

There I was, sitting in the back row at a clergy conference ignoring the speaker (who was actually pretty good). I remember hearing something about ministering in the community, reaching out to people in need, being a church for people who were not members—pretty good stuff, actually. But I was busy trying to balance the budget and at the same time figure out if we might have a shot at a capital campaign next year. The numbers weren't adding up—I was beyond frustrated. Why couldn't there be more? We needed more. Couldn't people see the need for more? Didn't they want to be more, for Jesus and each other?

Finally, it was break time, and people started moving. I joined the flow of people headed for coffee. I saw a colleague and friend I have known for twenty-plus years—he had just become a grandfather. I had heard that the baby had come very early. The family were asking for prayers but were cautiously optimistic.

We hugged, and I asked him how things were going. He smiled a wide and joyful smile, and said, "Tomorrow, I get to learn how to feed a preemie. How cool is that?" The joy and excitement of spending time with his grandchild was all over his face—he looked like a kid on Christmas Eve, waiting to open gifts.

He didn't need more because he had everything he could have asked for or imagined.

I walked quietly back to my seat and put away the budget. It was time to listen: Teach me, oh Lord, to want what is gifting, indeed.

—JASON LEO

❦

hunger builds up Lord
for more than
I need,

while others go
needing for less
than I crave.

may my fast be one
of the heart and
the body

teach me to want
what is gifting
indeed.

Wednesday, Lent I

From a distance, the world seems free of injustice and turmoil; our wilderness journeys seem to be a part of our past. Peace and harmony reign, and from a distance, all is well.

The things we hold at a distance become easily neglected: out of sight, out of mind. What is held at a distance only gives a partial view of a situation, where we present cups half full, instead of cups overflowing, to God. More importantly, when we respond to the challenges of life at a distance, we limit God's power from moving and operating through our lives.

Many times, even our best efforts will fall short of what is required or who we are required to be. In these uncomfortable spaces, may we remember we have a loving God who is mighty to save, protect, and redeem.

Whenever we feel detached or wander and stray, God will move mountains to find us, redirect us, and restore whatever we are lacking. May we work toward developing a personal relationship with our Creator—to not only know God from a distance but also close-up and personal—that we might experience the fullness of a loving and present God.

—Glenice Robinson-Como

Jesus Mary and Joseph
Moses Muhammad
and Buddha

the history books lie
when they leave
you out

as if all those lives
never found
life

or shaped the world,
in and through
you.

May I never forget
your name.

THURSDAY, LENT I

In movies and mythologies, we often see the protagonist face overwhelming odds and confront opponents with courage, only to be overcome. Whatever bravado the protagonist previously assumed is suddenly shattered. The noble and strong hero is forced to face the hard reality (perhaps for the first time) that he or she is not quite so noble, not quite so strong. And yet what looks like the end of the story proves to be a pivotal turning point. Those who are beaten down slowly, surely stand up. Those who have been overcome at last are overcomers.

This plot twist, a crucial shift in the story, comes not when the protagonist is securely in power but rather when the illusions of power, security, and control are finally surrendered. In his first letter to the Christians in Corinth, Paul warns the proud believers, "So if you think you are standing, watch out that you do not fall" (10:12). For his own part, Paul himself admits being plagued with an unspecified thorn in the flesh that was given to him, "to keep me from being too elated" (2 Corinthians 12:7).

How easy it is to fall from the heights of self-assurance to the depths of defeat and even despair. Yet as the apostle Paul went on to say to the Corinthians, "[Jesus] said to me, 'My grace is sufficient for you, for power is made perfect in weakness' (2 Corinthians 12:9)." When our own plot twists hit with hard reality, when our nobility and our strength prove insufficient for the needs of the present moment, then perhaps we will be ready to embrace new possibilities of divine grace. Perhaps at that point, we will humbly open ourselves to a power and love far greater than our own. Therein lies the blessed paradox of our life in Christ: When we recognize that God is God and that we are not—then and only then, shall we truly overcome.

—C. K. ROBERTSON

I find temptation to be
my teacher.

that I am not yet
as noble as I suppose
nor as strong,

yet you give me
another chance

to get it right today.

FRIDAY, LENT I

We live in a world that has spun away from holiness in pursuit of a long-lost, unrealistic dream of materialistic salvation. We are exposed to hatred that knows no bounds—proclaiming in city centers and town squares a message of vitriol and violence, seeing anyone who is different as "other."

We are tempted in this spun-out world to view every person we meet through a binary lens—love or hate, belief or unbelief, idealism or realism. That we might pit ourselves against one another in pursuit of a belief of rightness or goodness to save all humankind breaks the heart of the God who loves us enough to walk among us to show us a different way.

Jesus calls us to a new way, what the mystics call a third way — the way of the Trinity. This middle way is uninterested in being right or pious but is deeply invested in being righteous and in right relationship. We are called to be peacemakers in our own hearts and in the world.

This third way of being—this revolution of love and radical grace—saves the world and invites us to reclaim our soulful humanity. We come from a mighty spiritual lineage of countless feet walking through deserts, of strong voices rebuking temptation, of a carpenter king who walks into the world with a holy and powerful message of truth and grace clothed with flesh of an absolute and radical love.

—TERESA PASQUALE MATEUS

❧

our children's teeth are
set on edge by the
choices we have
made

that dollars and profits
are all that measure,
and souls
not.

turn us again to your
ways of wisdom,
recall our
hearts.

SATURDAY, LENT I

Philosopher George Steiner wrote that we live in a world "gone flat." He meant that we often feel as though there are no other dimensions than this—heaven and hell disappear—there is only this world, this moment. The collect for this week in Lent states in hope that God knows "the weaknesses of each of us, let each one find God mighty to save." What does that finding look like?

Perhaps it begins with discovering that the world is not flat, that there is a thin veil between this world and God's reality. Writer Paula D'Arcy says, "God comes disguised as your life." In other words, God is so mighty that God is with us in this world, even as God is beckoning us into the next. We are not waiting to experience the holy in the next world by merely enduring this one.

To press on in our journey of faith, especially during Lent, we must open our eyes, hearts, and lives to God's presence right now, in this present moment. Each Sunday, when we eat the bread and drink the cup, we claim our space in a multidimensional world—not a flat one. In those holy and consecrated moments, we are with Jesus at the Last Supper, surrounded by the great cloud of witnesses and in the present company of our worship community.

May we find God mighty to save by viewing and understanding the everyday parts of our lives as sacramental doorways to the holy. May we truly believe that "your presence is what truly feeds us each day." Let us pray this with all our hearts: May it be so.

—PORTER TAYLOR

❧

my family gathers around
like those at the table
in Jerusalem

when you took the bread
and said that you
would be with us.

we share a cup now
though not always
in remembrance

yet your presence is
what truly feeds us
each day.

may it be so.

THE SECOND WEEK IN LENT

Embraced and Held Fast

O God, whose glory it is always to have mercy: Be gracious to all who have gone astray from your ways, and bring them again with penitent hearts and steadfast faith to embrace and hold fast the unchangeable truth of your Word, Jesus Christ your Son; who with you and the Holy Spirit lives and reigns, one God, for ever and ever. Amen.

SUNDAY, LENT II

There is fierceness in denial, in refusing to tell the truth to ourselves, in refusing to acknowledge abuse and betrayal in our own lives. Still worse, we may minimize its shadow. Like stubborn toddlers, we tell ourselves "No. I will not drink from this cup. I will not have this thing that happened long ago impact me now."

Denial is the sweetest of temptations, because it closes our hearts and minds to our own grief, believing that we will gain some control over it. We say, "Time heals all wounds." But memories fluctuate and recycle, finding us again in unexpected hymns or the slant of sunlight through a window. When we deny ourselves the necessary and life-giving step of feeling our grief fully, we separate ourselves from the love of God.

When we refuse to accept the truth about our own lives, whatever reality we may be denying, we dissociate from our denial and our hurt by telling ourselves we are protecting those around us. Denying truth hinders our ability to be in right relationship with the world and with our loved ones in a variety of ways. While confronting the root and digesting the fruit of our pain and grief is a bitter experience, when we refuse to deny the truth, we may find that we are, in fact, embraced and held fast by a God who offers the unchangeable truth of love.

—CYNTHIA CANNON

Lord my heart rests
in you
at day's end

quiet comes to my
room

and I bow my head
in silent appreciation
for all
that filled my day

love, friends, warmth,
possibilities
and terrors alike.

may I not forget those
for whom
this day was more

difficult and trying, lonely
and hurtful

we are all in your hands.

Ashes and the Phoenix

MONDAY, LENT II

Less than a year after our daughter graduated from college, she came home, unable to find full-time work in a slow economy. For the next two-and-a-half years, she lived in her childhood bedroom, worked at temporary jobs, and spent many nights exploring the club scene. Despite having been an outstanding student, she felt like a failure. She was angry, frightened, confused, and depressed—as were her parents.

I bemoaned our situation to anyone who would listen. A friend responded with a story about an Ivy League college reunion. It was their tenth reunion, the tale goes, and the friends were comparing their successful careers when one asked about a woman who wasn't there.

"Oh," another said, "I heard she's come to a bad end—she's acting in pornographic films."

"A bad end," they all agreed, until one of the classmates suggested, "No—just a bad middle."

A bad middle...I found that concept tremendously comforting!

By the grace of God, our daughter (and her parents) survived a bad middle and have since moved on to happier times. But the "bad middle" is where we all are in this life—somewhere between the good creation God made us to be and the fulfillment of that intent in ways we can only imagine.

So we pray for grace, trusting in a God, "whose glory it is always to have mercy" to guide us through to a perfection we can't yet see.

—MARY W. COX

❧

if it is at all possible
let this cup pass
is our prayer

as we face opportunities
that challenge
but terrorize.

are we able, will we
fail, what if, what if

the hold backs that
eat at our hearts.

be with us to guide us
to hold and abide us,

our souls find their
center in thee.

—in honor of Patrick

Ashes and the Phoenix

TUESDAY, LENT II

I slipped into the pew next to my mom as the choir began processing down the aisle for Evensong. My father died a few years ago, and Evensong had been one of his favorite services. Normally, I enjoy the service, but on this night, for some reason, I felt nothing but grief and sadness—the kind I felt in the moments after his death, the type that hits like a brick.

The more beautiful the music was that night, the more I missed him. Unfortunately for me, the choir had apparently spent a lot of time in practice that week. A friend told me once, "The greater the darkness—the greater the possibility for light." Well, the sun was surely sinking that night, and I could feel the darkness of grief gathering around me.

The organ began to play the recessional hymn and my mother began to sing, "Abide with me, fast falls the evening tide…" She's not a very good singer, my mom, but she tries real hard.

The choir filed back down the aisle, followed by the altar party. One of the priests stopped next to my mom. He leaned over to her, murmuring just loud enough for me to hear, "I miss your husband. He was a good man." And then he moved on. I breathed out a huge exhale; that dark, heavy feeling of grief was lifted by just a few kind words and the knowledge that someone else missed him, too.

—JASON LEO

increase in me Lord
the gift
of humility

not the false hearted
t'weren't nothin'
t'weren't nothin'

nor the soul-harming
denial of value
to dare

but the truth-telling
knowledge
of both gifts and limit

that I may offer
the one
for the good and the
doing

and honor the other
for salvation from
despair.

Ashes and the Phoenix

Wednesday, Lent II

Heliotrope flowers, such as sunflowers, slowly turn their flowered faces during the day, continuously following the sun. These plants derive their name from the Greek words *helios*, meaning sun, and *tropos*, which means to turn. As heliotropes turn toward the sun, they develop strong roots and nutrients for longevity. Just as the sunflowers and their plant relatives are drawn to the sunlight for growth and development, so too should we be children of the light, a kind of "sonflower" drawn to the light of God for spiritual growth and development.

Yet too often we turn away from the true source of life, wrestling with the distractions of the world or our own pursuits. Perhaps we turn from Jesus because of our insecurities; perhaps we don't feel worthy.

The essence of Lent is an open invitation to turn our whole selves—our insides and our outsides—to bask in the love and light of a God who will never forsake us. Whenever we fall short of what we have been called to do and to be in the world, Jesus bids us to turn. The more we incline our hearts to God, the more our response to the true light becomes a natural response, something we don't even realize we are doing, just something we were made to do.

—Glenice Robinson-Como

for souls that have off wandered
for those who've never heard
for hearts that know but nothing
of what the faith has learned;

for peoples that have prospered
in only wealth of gold
but let the values soften
and turned their tone to scorn;

give mercy and forgiveness
but more Lord help us turn
to save us from a darkening
a world sore lost and burned.

Ashes and the Phoenix

THURSDAY, LENT II

How easy it is to be seduced by the myth that life is supposed to be easy. So, when things get hard—when relationships fragment, when illness strikes, when jobs are lost and paychecks cease—it is not surprising that we find our faith may wane or waver.

For some reason, we believe these disappointing things are not supposed to happen, at least not to us. When we fall into the seductive trap of assuming that smooth and steady are the norms—that life is supposed to be easy—it is no surprise that we are thrown into confusion and despair when we find reality quite different from the seductive lies we buy and sell daily.

There has long been a strain of Christianity that promises prosperity and an easy life if one only believes enough or is good enough. This simply isn't so—not based in reality or sound theology. How comforting it is to open up the Bible or *The Book of Common Prayer* and find in the Psalms a much more honest account of life. There, alongside comforting words like "The Lord is my shepherd, I shall not be in want" (23:1), we find cries such as, "My God, my God, why have you forsaken me?" (22:1).

Followers of Christ in every generation have learned firsthand that though God does not take away struggles that come our way, God does give us what we need to move forward—and moves with us. The key to a fulfilled life is not found on the smooth, glittering avenue of wishful thinking but rather on the unpaved, uneven highways and byways of real life to which God calls us and along which God journeys with us.

—C. K. ROBERTSON

❧

disappointments come when
least expected, over hopes
and plans much
anticipated

the readjusting of directions
the unwinding of feelings
can leave defeat in
the wake.

but then again they are a freeing from false
roads that would have
led astray.

may I find in their release
the space to find
pathways that
are true.

Friday, Lent II

Unknowing is one of the greatest gifts of the mystics, healers, and the hope-bearers among the people of faith. The absence of needing to have certainty, the lack of needing to be right—these are the two hands with which we hold the gift and challenge of unknowing.

Learning to hold unknowing helps us to understand that whatever knowledge and wisdom we accrue in this life— whatever we come to know—is a drop in the bucket of eternity, a glimpse at the reflection of truth through a dusty mirror, from a far-off vantage point. We are enlightened and encouraged by flickers of holiness in this life, and we hold onto them, tightly and rightly. Sometimes we hold fast to the reflection of holiness until our knuckles become white, forgetting that we are only holding a foggy reflection of truth. In our pursuit to know the unknowable, we choke out the light so we can see with our own desire. Let us find the wisdom to know that we do not know— as the Twelve Steps wisely remind us all. To remember that what we discover today may change in the light of new information we learn tomorrow.

Let us see that we cannot see it all—around all the edges and corners of creation and the mind of God. We must allow ourselves to be reminded daily of the wonder of the universe— of God exposing Godself to us through our lives and the world and the vast expanse of the whole of creation, without believing we will ever, or should ever, have all the answers. We will only continue to ask better questions, gazing up with wonder at the ineffable, repeating to ourselves, lest we forget, "I do not know." I must always remember to unknow, so that I might experience the intimacy of God without my own hubris getting in the way.

—Teresa Pasquale Mateus

misunderstandings test
us. can we say I'm sorry
or do we have to stand
and fall with our
perceptions.

help me Lord to stand
for what I believe, yet
to know that I may
not possess all
truth.

Aquinas after pages of
describing You had
the blessed humility
to end his words
'but not that.'

SATURDAY, LENT II

The word "Lent" means "to lengthen," and in the natural world, the days grow longer in this season. Our intention, in answering the Church's call to observe a holy Lent, is to grow in our awareness of God's goodness and mercy. As this awareness grows, God's grace and mercy call us to respond in faithfulness and thanksgiving. This is the true work of repentance.

We often mistake repentance for beating ourselves up over our sins and shortcomings—but that behavior and attitude are not pathways toward the light and love Jesus offers us with himself. One translation of the Greek word for repent is "to go beyond the mind you have." Our calling is to extend our vision so to glimpse God's glory and sense our true vocation as instruments for God's reign of peace, justice, and mercy. Then we respond with whole, contrite, and changed hearts.

When we repent, we stop thinking about ourselves—and what we can do—and we begin to think about God and what God has promised to do and is doing in our lives and in the world. When we do this, we notice the present blessings in our lives—the lovers and partners; a world that sings of wonder and grace; the magic of creation. We know that on our life journeys, we are held and embraced by God in the everydayness of our lives, and we are moved to give thanks, drawing our attention away from ourselves and toward the Giver. Thanksgiving awakens in us an awareness of being held and embraced by God, allowing us to release the death grip we have on our lives, so that instead of trying to manage our lives, we can simply live them for God.

—PORTER TAYLOR

❧

for lovers and partners
who bring smiles
to our faces
just because

for a world that sings
of wonder and grace
just walking
through

for pleasures and pains
that speak the intricate
magic of all creation
so direct

for my life and those
of all who have
been your
vehicles

I thank you, good Lord.

Ashes and the Phoenix

THE THIRD WEEK IN LENT

No Power in Ourselves to Help Ourselves

Almighty God, you know that we have no power in ourselves to help ourselves: Keep us both outwardly in our bodies and inwardly in our souls, that we may be defended from all adversities which may happen to the body, and from all evil thoughts which may assault and hurt the soul; through Jesus Christ our Lord, who lives and reigns with you and the Holy Spirit, one God, for ever and ever. Amen.

Ashes and the Phoenix

SUNDAY, LENT III

I am assaulted by anger. The unchangeable truth we live with is that we give things up all the time. We have given up so much, how can we be asked to do more? We have no power in ourselves to help ourselves, and that makes me angry.

In childhood, we gave up hope and joy in exchange for acceptance and safety. In old age, we give up our mobility, hearing, and eyesight, our senses of taste and smell. We move into retirement homes and grow small.

Oh yes, I am angry. Angry at God, and like David in the laments of the psalms, I will open my heart to let God hear my anger and hurt: *You never actually gave up your son! Oh, maybe for a weekend, but that's it. You have certainly made it so that we can walk in the way of his suffering. But what about you? Do you live in some parallel universe? I am always climbing the ladder! Where is the angelic heel I can grab hold of and wrestle to the ground for my blessing?*

From where I dwell, the storm is not at an end. I am wrestling with You, inside this storm, and I am hot and angry. I am wrestling, waiting for my blessing.

—CYNTHIA CANNON

deceits are all around us
closer than we know
or suspect.

harder to be let down
by those we thought
trustworthy, faithful

part of the community
part of your
name.

where the angels are
there demons will
be also

may we be innocent
as doves and wise
as serpents

as you advised us
when you first
came.

Ashes and the Phoenix

Monday, Lent III

Crutches often get a bad rap and are used as a metaphor for anything used to prop up someone weak or lazy. An addiction to drugs or food or shopping might be called a crutch. Sometimes we're even told, "Your religion is nothing but a crutch."

After foot surgery, crutches allowed me to function at work. I couldn't carry a cup of coffee across the office, but I was thankful to have them nevertheless. I learned that crutches aren't easy to use. They require balance, concentration, and significant upper-body strength. Stairs are generally impossible to navigate on crutches, and there's no way to carry anything that won't go in a backpack or hang around your neck.

Maybe faith is a crutch—we certainly need one, because there is no way we can save ourselves on our own. When I couldn't put my weight on my healing foot, I needed to learn to shift my weight to the crutches and trust that they would support me. That was hard, but my arms grew stronger, and I could walk by leaning on the crutches.

Learning to use the crutch of faith means building up the muscles of humility and trust. That, in turn, helps us to shift the weight of our sin and suffering to Jesus, who will support us, just as he carried his cross. It takes practice to walk on the crutch of faith, but if we ask, we have all the help we need.

—Mary W. Cox

suffering builds endurance,
which builds character,
which builds
hope

at least that is our hope
that we will not
just suffer
alone
without meaning.

your son is the living
voice of that hope
in his suffering
alone

that turned out to be
hope for the many,
the touch of
your hand

taking the worst
the world offers
transforming it to
good.
may it be so.

Ashes and the Phoenix

TUESDAY, LENT III

We all know the drill: Another bombing happens in some far away place, and we see the faces and bodies and parts of innocent victims who used to just be men, women, and children minding their own business. Inevitably, the militant, extremist, pseudo-religious, flavor-of-the-month terrorist group claims responsibility. Religious extremism and violence seem to be on the rise—as are religious indifference and apathy. What are we to say of these things? "Lord, have mercy," seems like a good place to start.

For twenty-five years, I have been involved in a ministry that provides affordable housing to low-income families. It's not a perfect solution to affordable housing, but it helps. One day, I was walking through the parish house and noticed that one of our priests was giving a tour to a Muslim woman, a member of a nearby mosque. I was kind of in a hurry—like I always am—but my clergy friend insisted on introducing me to this woman, explicitly sharing about my involvement in the housing ministry. Our Muslim guest looked at me immediately and said, "Our congregation would like to join you in this ministry. Would that be possible?"

There was no hesitation on her part and her directness indicated she was absolutely serious. I was amazed at the possibility of

Muslims and Christians working together for the common good. Maybe the kingdom really is at hand, really is between us, after all, just like Jesus says it is.

"Absolutely!" I responded. She smiled and there was, for a moment, light in a dark place, repair where there had only been breach, understanding where there had been only assumptions.

What then are we to say about these troubled times? "Lord, have mercy," is a good place to start—in despair, in times that are troubled indeed, but also surely in hope as well. The Spirit is moving in the hearts of people everywhere. Lord, have mercy. And praise the Lord, as God grants us mercy and shares it with us, among us, again and again.

—JASON LEO

༺༻

so many die too soon
too soon, yet nothing
went wrong

the mortality rate is
still one-hundred
percent

Lord, have mercy.

Ashes and the Phoenix

Wednesday, Lent III

In Jeremiah, God boldly proclaims to a beloved people, "For surely I know the plans I have for you...Plans for your welfare and not for harm, to give you a future with hope." These words reveal that it is God's desire and joy to provide a sense of comfort and security for the people of Judah. While their settlement in Babylon is extensive, they have grown weary and are filled with uncertainty. In these dark hours, it is difficult for the captives to envision the promises of a safe and secure future.

How often the scales on our eyes deceive us and limit our vision. When God stands with us on the mountaintops of life, we are at peace because God's activity among us is evident. But when we tread through the valleys of life, it is difficult for us to comprehend that God is also present among us.

In the midst of our struggles, we may find it difficult to imagine a God who is able to attend to our individual needs and the needs of all creation. God's activity in the world is an inclusive plan for the sanctity of all creation—the passage from Jeremiah says the *plans* God has for us. These plans—from God's great abundance—include a generous flow of blessings weaving their way throughout creation. Within these plans, we become one part of many. Within these plans, we experience the depth of God's care, which blesses, strengthens, and offers us grace and mercy.

—GLENICE ROBINSON-COMO

❧

taking a piece of the
truth as the whole
leads our hearts
astray

forgetting all the grace
that comes our way
as if only one part
mattered

help us to see your
hand beyond the
narrow focus of
our plans

THURSDAY, LENT III

Several years ago, I attended my son's baseball awards dinner. I walked over to a group of dads who were deep in conversation about the highlights of the season and introduced myself. One of them shook my hand and sheepishly admitted, "Oh, I thought your wife was a single parent." I tried to stammer out that my job kept me busy, but I was speechless upon realizing I had not been to a single game all season. It was a hard lesson in learning about what I say my priorities are and what they are in reality.

In his book, *Out of Solitude*, the late Henri Nouwen wrote of the importance of intentional solitude and prayer. "When we are able to create a lonely place in the midst of our actions and concerns, then our successes and failures slowly lose their power over us." Quality time with God, much like quality time with our family or friends, does not simply happen on its own. A conscious, deliberate choice is needed to make that time a priority…and not simply every now and then, or when I feel like it, or when I am finished doing what I consider to be more urgent or more important things. Only when we choose to pause and to see life through a different set of lenses will we find ourselves grounded in a power that is greater than our own and rediscover what is deeply real and truly important.

—C. K. ROBERTSON

let me rest in you
let me pause in you
let me see the day
through your eyes

and find peace.

Ashes and the Phoenix

FRIDAY, LENT III

One summer, I walked the Camino de Santiago, an ancient footpath for pilgrims in Northern Spain. It was an assault on the body and a test of the soul. But in the breaking down of body and soul, the Camino is not unique—life is the pilgrimage we walk.

This life ravages our bodies and our souls, and it tests us to the far corners of our sanity and the razor edge of our capacities. Life is lived upon a rugged path where we carry too much, walk much farther than we thought we could, encountering unexpected suffering and breathless beauty along the way. We find that we are all headed in the same direction, aimed toward the same destination, but walking in different ways and carrying different baggage.

Often this baggage separates us from one another, keeping us from seeing the truest self of the other. This is where the sacred can enter—into that space of uncertainty, disappointment, dysfunction, possibility, and growth. This is the dwelling place of the Holy Spirit, and it holds grace for the least of us in each of us, allowing us to see the truth at our cores. This sacred space, hallowed by the Spirit of God, allows us to release that which we can no longer carry in this life—sometimes our own baggage or perhaps the weight of another.

The blessed space of quiet discernment and contemplative understanding manifests itself when we are quiet enough to listen to the still, small voice guiding our path forward. When the Spirit speaks, we find and are found by companions who help us release what no longer serves the journey. We learn to let go and to move down the road, just a little farther—with love, grace, and honesty.

—Teresa Pasquale Mateus

❧

frustrations at others not
coming through in the
way we want
build barriers between us

making way for the limits
of others raises the
conundrum
do I encourage or settle
which way should I go.

may I have the wisdom
to know the one
from the other
and allow for your grace.

Ashes and the Phoenix

SATURDAY, LENT III

Sooner or later, all our tricks stop working. Our ways of managing our lives fall apart. Illusions of control dissipate—and there, at that most vulnerable and tender point, we fall into the hands of a living God. There is a reason Jesus has to enter the wilderness for forty days. In the River Jordan, Jesus hears God tell him that he is God's beloved, but Jesus still has to learn what this means. He has to learn that being God's beloved has nothing to do with power or position or prestige but is deeply rooted in trusting good—and the will of God—with all his heart.

Sooner or later, every one of us will find our way into the wilderness, discovering over and over again that we have no power in ourselves to help ourselves. Then, by God's grace, we turn around. We repent, we open our hearts to God. We ask God to come find us, because we do not know how to find where God is.

The real work of Lent is grounded in reorienting ourselves into right relationship with God. We don't need our worthiness of resurrection through mortification of the flesh or self-denial. Instead, we turn away from the illusion that we are in charge of anything except our intentions. In our turning to God, we ask to be connected to the source of our light and lives.

The men and women in the Bible who come closest to Jesus are those who have no illusions about their ability to make their lives work. They are lame, blind, bleeding, bereaved; some are even already dead. They have come to the end of their ropes and fall into the hands of the living God, praying the ultimate prayer of surrender and sacrifice, "Help."

In this season of Lent, may we have the honesty to admit our limitations and our brokenness. May we pray the prayer God always hears, "Help."

—PORTER TAYLOR

*have I spoken your name
enough*

*have I opened to speak
aloud*

what my heart believes

Jesus.

Ashes and the Phoenix

The Fourth Week in Lent

Give Us This Bread

Gracious Father, whose blessed Son Jesus Christ came down from heaven to be the true bread which gives life to the world: Evermore give us this bread, that he may live in us, and we in him; who lives and reigns with you and the Holy Spirit, one God, now and for ever. Amen.

SUNDAY, LENT IV

If only I had stayed with her the night she died alone in the hospital, maybe today I would be at peace with her death. Perhaps we could have had a moment of deep honesty together that would have brought healing to us both before she died. But instead, I was tired.

I went home and went to sleep. If only I hadn't been so selfish, that one time.

Surely, I could have stayed up with her that one night. It's too late now.

But Lord, do you think if I gave more to the homeless, or volunteered more hours, or went to church more often, do you think you could heal this torn place inside me? If I do more good works, will you make everything all right?

Lord, more than anything, I want one more chance.

I think I hear a rooster crowing.

—CYNTHIA CANNON

the air freshens like
your breath into
creation

over the waters
and into our
clay

life springing forth
with joy and
abandon

blessed be the
name of the
Lord today.

Ashes and the Phoenix

MONDAY, LENT IV

The League of Women Voters meeting was winding down. We finished our discussion of the issue at hand and came to a consensus on what position the League should take. The meeting adjourned, and we lingered over coffee, sharing our lives: laughing ruefully at things the husbands didn't quite understand, the dreadful messes toddlers managed to make. Suddenly, we became aware of the voice of the woman who had been our speaker, her voice cutting through our laughter: "I hate my husband."

Her husband, a prominent doctor, didn't care about her or their family, she said. One day—one of those days, full of minor household disasters and quarrelling children—he had come home, asking, "What's for dinner?" When she launched into her tale of woe, he had said, "Don't tell me about your day. I don't want to hear about your day."

"And," she told us, biting off the words, "I never told him about my day again."

There was stunned silence among us, and then a few awkward expressions of sympathy, and then we all went home, thinking about how frighteningly easy it is to starve a relationship. Years later, I saw that woman's name on the obituary page in the newspaper, and I wondered if she—or her husband—had ever relented, if she ever had brought herself to tell him about her day, and if he had listened, or if all their days together had ended in stony silence. We feed each other when we truly hear each other's stories, as God nourishes us with the bread of relationship, of listening and love.

—MARY W. COX

❦

our families open us
to joy, sorrow, pain
and laughter

like Mary and Joseph
Abraham and Sarah
we try to make a
way

following your star.

Ashes and the Phoenix

TUESDAY, LENT IV

My family visited a new church a couple of weeks ago, and there was no denying the awkwardness—like fish out of water. After worship, the youth group had a cake auction to raise money for a mission trip. Now, I'm not much on cake, but there were a couple of pies on the auction block. And I love pie. Things were looking up.

I had my heart set on a cherry one, but a woman across the room was a determined bidder, and eventually my family made me stop bidding. I was embarrassing them, allegedly.

I was still sulking over that cherry pie as we walked toward the car. From across the parking lot, I heard a loud shout. Here came the lady who stole my cherry pie, running toward us. Really? Was it time to rub it in that she had won the pie?

"Sorry about the pie! My daughter made it, and she said I had to buy it. But I have some homemade bread that I thought you might enjoy. I hope you come back."

Remember that part of the Lord's Prayer when we ask God to give us our daily bread? Well, that morning I missed out on a cherry pie, but we were offered some great bread, a good dose of grace, and the promise of new friends too.

—JASON LEO

*Spring waters flow
through the ice
sluice*

*like grace melting
away at my frozen
sins.*

*first a seep, then
a trickle, then
a roar*

*at the joy that flows
free when we
let it.*

Ashes and the Phoenix

WEDNESDAY, LENT IV

The Great Lancaster Textile Strike of 1912, often called, "The Bread and Roses Strike," is an example of the providence and purposes of God. The strike addressed unsafe working conditions and unequal pay for immigrant workers, many of whom were women and children. "Bread and Roses" became the slogan for the strike, as the women felt they were entitled to both bread and roses—fair pay and safe working conditions.

Throughout the scriptures, we hear many parables about meals, most involving bread. From the manna that fell from heaven to Jesus feeding the multitudes, bread serves as a symbol of God's providence in the world. Even today, the concept of the bread of life reminds us that God supplies our every need. But bread alone is more than what we consume—bread is so much more than a physical provision; it is a soul-transforming substance. The bread of life ensures that fair and equitable treatment is applied throughout the world. It ensures justice for "the least of these" and "forgives us our trespasses." Bread ensures that a seat at the table is intentionally provided for the uninvited and forgotten guest.

The bread of life enables us to recognize the God who nurtures our very being. When we ask for our daily bread, we are asking for the Holy Spirit to intervene to encourage healthy doses of discipline and unmerited mercy. Daily bread ensures that justice is scattered generously throughout all creation and that God's peace prevails on earth.

—GLENICE ROBINSON-COMO

❧

*I want to pray for
some who have
violated*

*friendships, faith,
community*

*but how can we forgive
in your name
when our hands and
hearts were not*

*among
the wounded.*

THURSDAY, LENT IV

Some seasons of life are full of twists and turns, bumps and detours. During such periods, we might want all the difficulty suddenly to evaporate, to click our heels three times, say the magic words, and find ourselves back in a more familiar and comfortable time. But as we well know, wishing things to be easier does not make them so. The hard truth is that "easier" does not even necessarily equal "better."

For more than twenty years, the U.S. Army ran a series of recruitment advertisements on television and at the movies, culminating in the memorable tagline, "Be all you can be." Images of soldiers engaging in extremely challenging and heroic endeavors flashed across the screen. This was no life of ease being presented to potential recruits. Instead, would-be soldiers were assured that they would be pressed to the limits of their abilities and beyond.

Normally advertisers, pundits, and politicians use promises of quick fixes or instant gratification. But this advertisement offered a very different message: sounding a call to stretch ourselves, to go beyond our capabilities and capacities, to have to try really hard. Anyone who has ever wanted to achieve a significant goal knows that it usually takes time and effort, often lots of effort, to reach the objective. Athletes, musicians, artists—anyone who has ever seen the prize several steps ahead—might very well ignore the pain and struggle it takes to get there.

As the apostle Paul once told the church in Corinth, like a runner he pressed on toward the goal in his faith and ministry. What Paul found, and what followers of Jesus are still discovering, is that God does not simply remove obstacles and problems. Instead, God gives us strength that we never knew we had to be all that God wants us to be, and offers us peace beyond our understanding to do what needs to be done. Those divine gifts, along with the support of others on the journey with us, present us with previously unimagined and unasked for possibilities. Thanks be to God.

—C. K. ROBERTSON

⌘

You give us tasks
that push and pull us
beyond our depths
and yet to our
deepest desires.

thank you for the gifts
that we do not call for
yet appreciate
when they have
arrived.

Ashes and the Phoenix

Friday, Lent IV

Desperation. Devastation. These feelings can shipwreck us on islands of pain and despair. We can be lost at sea, moored to dark, uncharted islands for what feels like centuries—even if the hurting time may be totaled only in minutes or hours.

We hold our pain close, like a lover. And we let it sink deep into us, like something sacred. It is easy to become stuck on this island of our own creation, wedded to our own pain. We cannot see outside ourselves, and we get lost in the thick fog of grief that covers the ground and fills the air. If we stay on this island of hurt long enough, we lose the ability to see beyond our own body to even know how to begin to escape.

The one bread, the one body that has been broken for us and extravagantly shared with us is the reminder of life eternal— reminding us that we can live lives beyond the pain, suffering, and betrayals the world deals us. The one bread reminds us to leave that island—and Jesus, as the guide who clears the path through the fog, helps us find the way out of despair.

Death can seem insurmountable—the metaphorical deaths we suffer, the end of relationships, plans gone awry, hopes faded and forgotten. Yet this bread, this sacred bread, is the arm outstretched, pulling us out of the darkness, out of the pain, and into new life. We consume this holy bread and are nourished with rebirth in every breath, every bite, every realization that the fog of grief and the island of suffering and the storms of this life are not eternal.

All that is eternal is the life offered in this one bread, this one body, broken for us.

—TERESA PASQUALE MATEUS

❧

storms come back
around, like life
crashes

we thought were over
but weren't.

protect us Lord from
despair, defeat, from
going under

when we are most
vulnerable at the
end of

frayed hopes.

Ashes and the Phoenix

Saturday, Lent IV

Catherine of Siena, doctor of the Church and scholastic theologian, said, "All the way to heaven is heaven, and all the way to hell is hell." Holding the intention of this phrase in our hearts reminds us that we taste the bread of heaven at each celebration of the Holy Eucharist. Even as we live in expectation of the day when all the faithful are gathered together at God's heavenly banquet, we have a foretaste of that feast here and now. It's why at the Ascension, the angels ask the disciples, "Why do you stand looking up toward heaven?"

In some sense, we have yet to comprehend the radical news of the Incarnation. "And the Word became flesh and lived among us" (John 1:14a). If we want to see God's presence, it will be "in faces and places...smiles and cries...amidst us all." We must stop thinking of God as an other-worldly entity and be open to seeing God reveal the divine presence in us and all around us.

The other world is not in some far away place, but rather is found by simply altering our perception. We see what we are looking for. During this Lent, let us look for Christ in the ordinariness of our lives and in the faces of the people we encounter. Let us be open to the other world, which is the world of grace and the kingdom the Lord asks us to seek.

—PORTER TAYLOR

give me a heart to
see your hand

in faces and places
smiles and cries

in anguish and
anger

hope and help

the fact of your
presence

amidst us all.

The Swift and Varied Changes of the World

Almighty God, you alone can bring into order the unruly wills and affections of sinners: Grant your people grace to love what you command and desire what you promise; that, among the swift and varied changes of the world, our hearts may surely there be fixed where true joys are to be found; through Jesus Christ our Lord, who lives and reigns with you and the Holy Spirit, one God, now and for ever. Amen.

SUNDAY, LENT V

More than anything, I want to sit with my own dead, those who have left me with only black holes of nothingness in my universe. Why has life forsaken me? Where is the daily bread we have been promised?

I look at the news and read the headlines. I look at my friends who suffer emotionally and physically. I look at the mentally ill in my own family, who, without financial support from us, would be homeless. I know others are sitting near me in pews, or on buses, or in uncomfortable office chairs who are also suffering, alone in their grief.

Is it finished? Are we finished?

Be not far from me, for trouble is near, and there is none to help.

—CYNTHIA CANNON

how'm I doin' the
mayor said

am I living up to
what you had in
mind

am I letting down
the side

or surprising you
with my wit.

how'm I doin'
I ask the Lord

am I living up to
what you had
in mind

holding up my part
for the side

using my best wits
to move the game

how'm I doin'
dear Lord

on who
I can become

Ashes and the Phoenix

MONDAY, LENT V

God knows we need dreams—not only the visions that stream through our unconscious minds when we sleep but also our seemingly frivolous daydreams.

When I was a teenager, I would fantasize about going to Hollywood and winning awards. I was not an actor, but I thought I might write a brilliant screenplay that would merit an Oscar as a crowning achievement for my creative gifts.

Nearly fifty years later that dream came true—in a way. The Episcopal Communicators held their annual conference in Los Angeles, and the awards banquet was at a venue in Hollywood, where I received several awards for our diocesan publications. I told my friends that God must have laughed. I had dreamed of the glamour, applause, and adulation of a red-carpet experience, but God had something better in mind.

The true prize was that I had been led through many "swift and varied changes" to a place where I was using my gifts as I believe God intended: sharing the good news of the Spirit's work among the people of our diocese and celebrating the ministries of faithful disciples. In our dreams, through our dreams, and out of our dreams, our hearts are constantly drawn toward the true joys of God's dream for us and for all creation.

—MARY W. COX

quiet. night. silence moving about
while our minds weave in
and out, dreaming our ways
into tastes of something we
cannot express.

you come to us in dreams.

of wheat stalks, of angels and ladders
to heaven, of fat and thin cows,
and blankets filled with forbidden
foods descending

while voices tell us
to take and eat,
to take the child and flee,
to take heart.

come to the windows
of our dreams again
now where night opens
the portals and we
resist no more
your movings in
our soul.

Ashes and the Phoenix

TUESDAY, LENT V

A good friend worked as a traveling salesman for many years. One night, a truck made a sudden left-hand turn in front of him, and in an instant he was as close to death as you can be—one foot in the already, another in the not-yet. The wreck was brutal.

After months of recovery and rehab, he decided to go back to school—it was time for a new career. School was far from home, and he knew no one in this new place, so he joined a church. The building was in a downtown area, and he noticed right away that the neighborhood kids and the church kids had nowhere to play.

On his own, my friend raised money for a playground at the church, asking for volunteers from the parish to help build it. One of the women at the church was so impressed with his commitment that she volunteered to help with the construction. They fell in love and soon were married. Their third child was baptized a few weeks ago.

The swift and varied changes of this world are disconcerting—they make us uncomfortable and stressed. But they are not all bad. Sometimes, the earth has to shake a little for us to stumble our way into the kingdom.

Mindful that God is doing more for us than we could ever ask or imagine, we continue on the journey set before us. We carry on and persevere, trusting in God's never-failing goodness and mercy, even as we long to glimpse the kingdom of God where all true joys are to be found, even in the midst of the swift and varied changes of this world.

—Jason Leo

*in the garden a
knowledge was
sought*

*that we could not
deal with*

*of good and evil
not as measures*

but from the inside.

*that dark knowing
breaks us still.*

deliver us please

from temptation.

Ashes and the Phoenix

WEDNESDAY, LENT V

We face a multitude of issues from the misuse of "this fragile earth, our island home." From global warming to the depletion of natural resources, environmental neglect has caused waves of destruction throughout the entire world. In the book of Genesis, humans are given God's blessing of dominion over the earth—established not to exploit our resources but to understand the interconnectedness between our lives and the earth. In responding to the constant changes in and across many cultures and millennia, our lifestyles have greatly influenced (and continue to influence) the health and sanctity of our environment. Somewhere along our way, we lost sight of how the earth nourishes and sustains us.

As trustees of God's good creation and all that lives upon the face of the earth and beneath the surface of the waves, we are called to reclaim our care of creation and to develop a deeper awareness and respect of the earth, working diligently to prevent further environmental harm. More importantly, it is our responsibility to begin to envision new possibilities to preserve the earth. We must begin to make daily choices that will assure future generations a more sustainable world. Sister Joan Chittister says, "We are each called to go through life reclaiming the planet an inch at a time until the Garden of Eden grows green again."

As we begin this process of "re-greening the earth," we begin to resurrect the original narrative of God's plan and intentions for the whole of creation. If we truly love the Creator, we will develop innovative practices that demonstrate our love of creation. The earth is continuously groaning for care and nurture. The earth is groaning—even now—but are we listening?

—GLENICE ROBINSON-COMO

brothers and sisters
saints wait

for the unveiling of
new eyes

that see what they
see

new worlds possible
with grace.

Lord I want to be in
that number

when the saints...

THURSDAY, LENT V

It had been a particularly difficult day: Everyone seemed to need me—to say the perfect words, to do the helpful thing. And for the most part, I felt like I kept coming up with a big zero, that I couldn't say or do anything right. I was exhausted, weighed down.

As I walked into the office at the end of the day, my assistant took one look at me and in a sing-song voice said, "I hadn't heard the news!" My response was short and sharp, "What news?" Her smile met my grimace, and my assistant (who was not above a touch of sarcasm) quietly said, "The news that God resigned, and you have been named the replacement."

This reminder that God is God and I am not is good news for those of us who struggle to hold it together in the midst of the changes and chances of this life, striving always to be responsive and responsible. "Come to me," Jesus calls, "all you that are weary and are carrying heavy burdens, and I will give you rest."

You and I—we don't have to keep juggling everything perfectly all the time. We don't have to wake up each day and worry about whether we will get it all right. We don't have to go to sleep each night regretting all the ways we failed others and ourselves. No, God has not resigned. God never will.

We are indeed called to be responsive and responsible, but we are also called to maintain a healthy perspective. God is God, not you, not me. We are God's children, who don't always perform perfectly but who are always perfectly loved.

—C. K. ROBERTSON

*connections opened when
we first stopped hiding
first stopped running
from the truth that
we are not*

the center.

*and opened
conversation with
you, the Other, who
led us to an Other, thru
whom we came to know
each other, and our selves.*

Friday, Lent V

We are both eternal and finite. In soul we are eternal. In body we are finite. To hold this duality is impossible—without the intervention of divinity. We must be able to hold the tension of what the contemplatives call the both-and phenomenon. We must be able to live in the tension of being both body and spirit, both finite and eternal. To do so means living into the life we have now, and also understanding that everything that is will pass away, and only matters for today.

To fight for justice, to love with authenticity, to have compassion toward all people, and to strive to be the greatest version of ourselves has value and worth but is also temporary and finite. If we can hold the tension of knowing and remembering—from a cellular to a spiritual level—that it is all temporary, we can live into each day fully, without being too attached to the seriousness of the present or the outcome of our strife. We fight no less. We try no less. We aspire no less. We love no less. We give everything, and then we let it go. We let it go. We let it go. We give all we can in this life, and then we let it go.

—Teresa Pasquale Mateus

in the last days we

seem to cry

about things that

have not gone well

in our lives

as if we were supposed

to be immune from

the gifts you gave us of

mortality and limits

as if my body was not

joy enough even if not

forever, nor my soul

meant for more.

Ashes and the Phoenix

SATURDAY, LENT V

There's a story of a young monk who proudly came to the Abbott to show off his piety. He told the elder of his many prayer practices, his great knowledge of the scripture, and his correct observance of fasts and holy days. When he was finally silent, the Abbott gave him an empty glass and began pouring water into it. Although the glass became full, the Abbott kept pouring. As the water spilled on the floor, the young monk cried, "Stop, there's no room for anymore." "Yes," said the elder. "Go and empty your glass so that you have room for the Lord."

This is how it is with us: God does not want our frantic activity or our many accomplishments. God wants us. All of us. God wants our devotion, attention, and love. Christianity is not a contest for the faithful to show off their spiritual merit badges. Christianity is a love affair.

Lent is a time to be still and know that God is God, opening ourselves to the radical grace God wants to shower upon us. Among these swift and varied changes of the world, may "our hearts…surely…be fixed where true joys are to be found."

—PORTER TAYLOR

purity of heart, said
Kierkegaard, is to
will one thing

but I do not, and the
tear rends me with
confusion.

quiet my heart
O Lord

that I may see your
path forward and
let be.

Walk in the Way of His Suffering

Almighty and everliving God, in your tender love for the human race you sent your Son our Savior Jesus Christ to take upon him our human nature, and to suffer death upon the cross, giving us the example of his great humility: Mercifully grant that we may walk in the way of his suffering, and also share in his resurrection; through Jesus Christ our Lord, who lives and reigns with you and the Holy Spirit, one God, for ever and ever. Amen.

Acceptance is not being free of anger or fear, nor is it about being joyous. Acceptance is about optimum function—coping with the deep grief we all live with. We are all drawn to the foot of the cross. The suffering is ours; we are nowhere near finished with our work. But like Jesus in his final moments, we must look outward at those around us—at all the others next to us, in the pews and cities where we live.

Hanging on the cross, Jesus looks at his family and friends and the community that is being eviscerated. But instead of despairing, he quietly puts it back together again with an act of mercy, by entrusting the care of his mother and friends to one another, by sowing the seeds of a new community just beginning to take shape. The community that is birthed and nourished by Jesus' great act of compassion and mercy is not just about bloodlines—it is a community to which we all belong.

Our job is to accept life, this and every moment in life, even as life breaks our hearts in deep and difficult ways. We push away radical acceptance, deny it, get angry at, bargain with, feel depressed about, and grieve over—but acceptance opens us up to compassion. When we eat of the fruit of the bitter tree of this mortal life, the only remedy we are offered is the enlargement of compassion. And compassion is the only thing that saves the world. *Tikkum Olam*

—CYNTHIA CANNON

we cheered you on
especially when we
thought it would go
our way

but when it didn't
follow our script
we turned
and still do.

forgive us our stupidity,
cupidity, rapidity,
done-deedity.

we don't make it
home
without you.

Ashes and the Phoenix

MONDAY IN HOLY WEEK

The Way of Life and Peace

Almighty God, whose most dear Son went not up to joy but first he suffered pain, and entered not into glory before he was crucified: Mercifully grant that we, walking in the way of the cross, may find it none other than the way of life and peace; through Jesus Christ your Son our Lord, who lives and reigns with you and the Holy Spirit, one God, for ever and ever. Amen.

On Palm Sunday last year our choir sang a passionate setting of *Solus ad victimam*—an English translation by Helen Waddell of a medieval Latin poem by Peter Abelard. "Alone to sacrifice thou goest, Lord," it begins, and quickly gets to the tough part: "For they are ours, O Lord, our deeds, our deeds. Why should thou suffer torture for our sin?"

This where I often get stuck in Holy Week—wallowing in my sins, my shame, my utterly vile and unworthy self. Of course that's just the problem—suddenly it's all about me. Cross purposes indeed!

If the cross is to mean anything, it is not about our guilt and shame but rather fundamentally about the incomprehensible love of God. The Creator of all that is became a human creature—hungry, thirsty, weary, confused, and tempted, like us. And this God-incarnate, man-Divine is tortured, suffering appalling physical pain and humiliation, the soul-shattering pain of betrayal, and the cold emptiness of perceived abandonment by God. And this beautiful Jesus dies. "Giving himself to Death, whom he hath slain," Abelard's poem says.

The Son of God dies at the hands of people exactly like us because he loves us. I cannot begin to wrap my mind around this thought. Every year, I think how much easier it would be simply to look away from this incredibly visceral and vulnerable act of surrender and total love. But I can't. I can't look away because I believe that if we walk with Jesus through this week of suffering, just as he walks with us through our own pain, we will find the path of sacrifice to also be the way of life and peace.

Death never has the last word—Abelard's poem ends with, "the laughter of thine Easter Day." That's where this week's road leads.

—MARY W. COX

❦

*on the steps to the cross
there were stumbles
not by you but by us.*

*mixed signals, cross
purposes, bad karmas
how could we miss
your loving so clear.*

*mixed signals, cross
purposes, bad karmas
our answers were wanting
our visions unclear.*

TUESDAY IN HOLY WEEK

To Glory in the Cross of Christ

O God, by the passion of your blessed Son you made an instrument of shameful death to be for us the means of life: Grant us so to glory in the cross of Christ, that we may gladly suffer shame and loss for the sake of your Son our Savior Jesus Christ; who lives and reigns with you and the Holy Spirit, one God, for ever and ever. Amen.

A friend was in the final days of battling cancer. Death was around the corner. But the strength of her faith and hope in the future—even in her own future—was amazing. She said, "I have every reason to be optimistic." I smiled, and she yelled at me and called my smile condescending and trite. She was right.

So I asked her about her hope and optimism and where it came from. Her words stay with me, "It is a scientific impossibility that nothing created everything and that life sprang from non-life. There must be a higher being and that is where I am going, who I am journeying to." And then we both smiled.

Jesus' journey to the cross is awful. To read the account in the scriptures is an unavoidably sad experience because we see into his pain and suffering. It is an awful journey, and there is no denying it. But there is more going on in the story of Holy Week besides Jesus' death, more going on than a horrible story of the execution and death of a good man. It is the beginning of a journey to new life for Jesus and for us—for all of us.

Thank God Jesus does not quit, that his journey continues, and that ours does too. Thank God, Jesus walks and talks until the very end, breathing the breath of life so that we too can continue our journey—so that we might breathe along with him in this world and in the age to come, have life everlasting.

—JASON LEO

endings come upon us,
valleys of dry bones
loom

how will our bones rise
from deceit and lies
and greed

when we have gone
to the dust, refusing
to listen

breathe your breath
into us, re-sinew
us

while there is still
time.

Ashes and the Phoenix

Wednesday in Holy Week

Give Us Grace

Lord God, whose blessed Son our Savior gave his body to be whipped and his face to be spit upon: Give us grace to accept joyfully the sufferings of the present time, confident of the glory that shall be revealed; through Jesus Christ your Son our Lord, who lives and reigns with you and the Holy Spirit, one God, for ever and ever. Amen.

Throughout our earthly lives, troubled waters may leave us feeling abandoned. Desperate options present empty opportunities and lead us to question our faith and our God. In our despair, we cry out, "Abba, why me? Why now?" These questions plague our thoughts, leaving us feeling lost and alone. The discomfort of suffering can evoke a spirit of fear and a sense of rejection. Fear places limits on our faith, and when our faith is limited, we limit our God. When we question the "whys" of the stony paths we encounter in life, we also question God's justice.

Matthew tells us that when Jesus goes to pray in the Garden of Gethsemane, his petition is for God to change the course of what Jesus knows is about to happen. In these very words, Jesus exemplifies profound vulnerability with God, expressing his deepest fears but also his deepest trust in God. At various points throughout my life, I have asked God, "Why this? Why now? Why me?" and I have learned that the lesson and blessin' lies within and through the journey.

"Mother to Son," a poem by Langston Hughes, has always inspired me in my wilderness journeys. In this poem, the mother describes her journey to her son in this way, "Life for me ain't been no crystal stair. It's had tacks in it and splinters. But all the time I'se been a climbin'." We all encounter stones along the journey of life, but our faith will sustain us along the rocky roads. Our journeys will certainly become rugged and uncomfortable in places, but if we are faithful, they will transform our lives. Whenever we encounter the broken and

Ashes and the Phoenix

stone-ridden parts of life's pathway, may we each remember to "keep climbin." God will meet us wherever we are and will provide sustenance through our driest deserts.

Keep climbin'.

—GLENICE ROBINSON-COMO

❦

we come to red seas
of our own devising
the pains and chains
of a lifetime crowding
us up against the
sands of desperation

until we turn and see
your hand swiping
wide the waters to
lead us home on dry
ground

give us grace
to turn
and take the path.

MAUNDY THURSDAY

These Holy Mysteries

Almighty Father, whose dear Son, on the night before he suffered, instituted the Sacrament of his Body and Blood: Mercifully grant that we may receive it thankfully in remembrance of Jesus Christ our Lord, who in these holy mysteries gives us a pledge of eternal life; and who now lives and reigns with you and the Holy Spirit, one God, for ever and ever. Amen.

Since the first Passover, friends and fellow pilgrims come together by candlelight for a quiet meal. They break bread, share wine, sing hymns, and remember the divine covenant through which the God of compassion came to the aid of an enslaved and fearful people—redeeming and restoring them.

Why then should the Passover meal in the Upper Room, shared by Jesus and those closest to him, be any different? Familiar hymns are sung and the familiar prayers are prayed. But then, just as the bread is broken, Jesus surprises everyone gathered by sharing a new understanding about the bread and the cup. No longer do we hear, "This is the bread of the Passover," but rather, "This is my body." Nor do we hear, "This is the wine of the old covenant," but rather, "This is my blood of the new covenant, for the forgiveness of sins."

This night with Jesus and his companions is a night of drama—of betrayals, denials, and total abandonment. This is a night of tears, accusations, and utter aloneness. This is a night that only grows darker with the coming day—it is a night of gloom and impending death.

Yet, before all of this, in that candlelit room, our beloved Friend proclaims to all of us that, more than anything else it may or may not be, this is a night of unequivocal, unlimited, unending love. In this new covenant, our dear Friend promises to hold us close, to lead us through the valley of the shadow of death, to redeem and restore each and every last one of us anew.

—C. K. ROBERTSON

the maundy's mandates
call us again

to remember by doing
to recall by caring

bread, wine, feet, souls
the simplest things

for telling the most elegant
of stories.

Ashes and the Phoenix

Holy Week

GOOD FRIDAY

Behold This Your Family

Almighty God, we pray you graciously to behold this your family, for whom our Lord Jesus Christ was willing to be betrayed, and given into the hands of sinners, and to suffer death upon the cross; who now lives and reigns with you and the Holy Spirit, one God, for ever and ever. Amen.

We are the human family and we are all part of one body. We see many things we find hard to look at, too painful or too grotesque. But we also see the things we find beautiful, radiating so much light that we sometimes squint at the brightness, finding it difficult to look directly into the face of loveliness.

We have an incredible capacity to be both our worst and our best parts—in each of our hearts and across the wide expanse of the human family. We are, even in all our mess, the beloved community—God's family. We are all part of the body that Jesus comes to save and will one day resurrect into our fullest, best expressions.

We must believe we are part of this body—the light and the dark, the good deeds and the bad. We are no more perfect or imperfect than any other part, although sometimes we reflect more shadow than light. We are all part of the body, a body saved from its own self by the eternal and unending love of sacrifice. This profound and unfathomable divine love is exactly what Jesus comes to remind us about—we are both the very best and very worst, and we are all worth saving.

Whenever we forget this—whether we are forgetting ourselves, our neighbors, the other people in our lives—Jesus asks us to remember that we are all worth saving. Let us live this truth.

—Teresa Pasquale Mateus

robbery, rape, murder
treason, theft, cruelty

mean kids bullying the
weak, strong kids
pushing their weight

a mother beating a
vulnerable child,
a father violating
their innocence

when we are at our
most despicable,
totally inexcusable

you died for
our sins.

HOLY SATURDAY

The Third Day

O God, Creator of heaven and earth: Grant that, as the crucified body of your dear Son was laid in the tomb and rested on this holy Sabbath, so we may await with him the coming of the third day, and rise with him to newness of life; who now lives and reigns with you and the Holy Spirit, one God, for ever and ever. Amen.

Sometimes, it feels like the world is on a repetitive, circular-action loop. Today feels like yesterday, and in our quiet despair, we believe tomorrow will be the same. Our world and our expectations become very small. We dare not hope for too much nor think of a future radically different from the present moment. Nations will continue to wage war; terrorists will continue to tyrannize people's hearts and lives.

However, this Saturday night is not just any old regular Saturday night. This is the Passover of the Lord. On this night, everything that cannot happen happens. Those who have been marked for death are given new life. In response to this Passover miracle, God's people are invited to embrace all the hopes they have fearfully stored away and invited to begin their journey to a new future. This Saturday brings a new world. It seems impossible, beyond our belief. But the events of this night are real. And nothing in the world or in our lives will ever be the same.

On this night, a night different from all others, we dismiss our cynical doubts about God's power and ability to make us and this world new. We discard any distrust we have in God's power and embrace this miraculous deliverance from the old life of slavery and bondage into a covenant with the living God.

—PORTER TAYLOR

❧

Ashes and the Phoenix

on a night like tonight
people passed over

from a land filled with suffering
to a place of new heart.

on a night like tonight
the wild avenging angel

struck down the arrogance
of a people of blood

on a night like tonight
death gave its last gasp

of trying to hold the
One who'd been killed.

on a night like tonight
we all were brought over

to a place of new promise
for a life of fresh starts.

Holy Week

The Gate of Everlasting Life

Almighty God, who through your only-begotten Son Jesus Christ overcame death and opened to us the gate of everlasting life: Grant that we, who celebrate with joy the day of the Lord's resurrection, may be raised from the death of sin by your life-giving Spirit; through Jesus Christ our Lord, who lives and reigns with you and the Holy Spirit one God, now and for ever. Amen.

Hallel: Hebrew, to praise
u: Second person plural imperative form
jah: ending for the sacred name: Jahweh/Yahweh/YHWH

I had said and praised and shouted, "Hallelujah," for years before I realized exactly what it meant. Not until my Greek and Hebrew classes in seminary did I learn that Hallelujah—or the Anglicized "Alleluia"—was a shout of praise to the specific living LORD, Jah—the God of Abraham and Sarah, Isaac and Rebekah, Jacob and Leah and Rachel.

So, let us praise the LORD, the One of the Sacred Name, revealed to Moses in the burning bush, made manifest to the people of Israel at Passover and deliverance at the Red Sea, carved into hearts and minds through the gift of the commandments, abiding in companionship and succor in the pillars of fire and cloud, and wonderfully incarnate in the gift of the Sacred Son—the Beloved who dies and rises for us—the incomparable gift of the One with that other sacred name—Jesus the Christ.

Let our praises rise to the One who has, through the years revealed Godself—beyond all gender—to us. Thank you God, for all of it—the dark moments when light has been needed, amid the desolations and denials when forgiveness has been all we could pray for, in deliverances and births and new, unearned moments of grace—from all those possibilities from which our prayers and praises of, "Thank you. Praise you!" have sprung up—we thank you for putting the reasons for thanks in our lives and for sending the words leaping from our hearts.

Praise God—God who is caring—just, loving, personal, gracious, forgiving, creating. God who is One. We praise you with our whole hearts.

And perhaps, most importantly, we praise this living God who is victorious, who, in the victory of our Lord Jesus Christ, rises from the ashes, a phoenix in triumph over the forces of death and evil.

We serve and praise a God of truth, and one of the true facts about this life is that we are all born to die. And this would be true, except for the truth of the resurrection, which turns all that is evil on its head and reveals the most basic and formative emotion for our lives: Hope.

Hallelu-JAH, indeed.

—LEN FREEMAN

❧

Hallelu-jah.

Hallelu-jah.

Hallelu-JAH.

Ashes and the Phoenix

THE POET

LEONARD FREEMAN recommends writing a poem and taking a walk every day for a disciplined, balanced life. A retired Episcopal priest and journalist, Len has worked at Trinity Wall Street and Washington National Cathedral, along with several other wonderful parishes. He has published a number of works over the years, including video series, film, and media reviews. His most recent poetry offerings, *Hawai'i: Poems from a Promised Land* and *Safe in a Tree, Imara and Me,* are available from Amazon.com. Along with his wife Lindsay, Len has written *Good Lord, Deliver Us,* published by Forward Movement.

THE ARTIST

JASON SIERRA is a designer and visual artist based in Washington, D.C. His art brings together Christian symbols, Mexican-American folk art, and a post-colonial worldview. He works in management consulting for the Boston Consulting Group and spends his weekends making things.

THE CONTRIBUTORS

MARY W. COX retired in 2012 as director of communications for the Diocese of Southeast Florida. She lives in Charlotte, North Carolina, where she and her husband enjoy singing in the choir at Church of the Holy Comforter. She writes light verse and haiku and takes a camera on her daily walks, practicing to become a more skilled photographer. She is a frequent Forward Movement collaborator, including contributions to several editions of annual devotions.

JASON LEO is an Episcopal priest and serves as missioner for congregational vitality for the Diocese of Southern Ohio. His vocational career has carried him across oceans, up mountainsides, and all the way back home to the Ohio Valley, where he makes his home with his wife and their three children. Jason is an enthusiastic contributor to Forward Movement resources.

GLENICE ROBINSON-COMO serves as canon pastor of Christ Church Cathedral in Dallas, Texas. A native Virginian, she received an M.Div. from Perkins School of Theology at Southern Methodist University and a diploma of theological studies from the Episcopal Theological Seminary of the Southwest. She worked as a staff ombudsman with the Houston-Galveston Area Agency on Aging for ten years, in contract administration with the Department of Defense, and with the Metropolitan Transit Authority in Southern California. Glenice is the chair of the Commission on Black Ministry, a member of the diversity committee at the Seminary of the Southwest, a board member of Amazing Place, and a trained facilitator for Veriditas labyrinths. She and her husband have two children.

C. K. ROBERTSON serves as canon to the presiding bishop of The Episcopal Church and as a distinguished visiting professor at General Theological Seminary in New York City. A member of the Council of Foreign Relations, he also serves on the board of the *Anglican Theological Review* and is general editor of the *Studies in Episcopal and Anglican Theology* series. Chuck has authored more than a dozen books (www.ckrobertson.com) and was featured in Forward Movement's *Abiding with God Day by Day.*

TERESA PASQUALE MATEUS wears many hats, including author, trauma specialist, educator, trainer, yoga teacher, and a meditation and retreat facilitator. She advocates on behalf of women who have been victims of violence and marginalized people and works in a variety of ways to address these issues, including participation and leadership related to organizations such as TransFORM Missional Network, Wild Goose Festival, and Episcopal Peace Fellowship. She also was a leader in developing the Repudiation of the Doctrine of Discovery. She is founder and co-curator of the Voices Out of Darkness initiative and annual gathering to bring awareness and support around issues of addiction, trauma, and suicide. She has previously contributed to *Abiding with God Day by Day*, published by Forward Movement.

PORTER TAYLOR retired as the sixth bishop of the Diocese of Western North Carolina in 2016. In the fall of 2017 he will join the faculty of the Wake Forest University School of Divinity. He was ordained to the priesthood in 1994 and was consecrated as bishop in 2004—the 999th bishop to have been consecrated in The Episcopal Church. Porter leads retreats and is the author of *To Dream as God Dreams: Sermons of Hope, Conversion, and Community* and *From Anger to Zion: An Alphabet of Faith*. He and his wife Jo have two children. They currently make their home in North Carolina.

**CYNTHIA CANNON** is the executive director for the Consortium of Endowed Episcopal Parishes. Prior to her work with the consortium, she worked at Lawrence Hall Youth Services, the largest child welfare agency in the state of Illinois. Before coming to Lawrence Hall, she worked for Episcopal Charities and Community Services in Chicago where she coordinated special events and publications. Cynthia has an extensive background in writing, event planning, and association management. Cynthia and her husband and their three cats live happily in a Victorian home in San Antonio, Texas.

ABOUT FORWARD MOVEMENT

Forward Movement is committed to inspiring disciples and empowering evangelists. While we produce great resources like this book, Forward Movement is not a publishing company. We are a ministry.

Our mission is to support you in your spiritual journey, to help you grow as a follower of Jesus Christ. Publishing books, daily reflections, studies for small groups, and online resources is an important way that we live out this ministry. More than a half million people read our daily devotions through *Forward Day by Day*, which is also available in Spanish (*Adelante Día a Día*) and Braille, online, as a podcast, and as an app for your smartphones or tablets. It is mailed to more than fifty countries, and we donate nearly 30,000 copies each quarter to prisons, hospitals, and nursing homes. We actively seek partners across the Church and look for ways to provide resources that inspire and challenge.

A ministry of The Episcopal Church for eighty years, Forward Movement is a nonprofit organization funded by sales of resources and gifts from generous donors. To learn more about Forward Movement and our resources, please visit us at ForwardMovement.org (or VenAdelante.org).

We are delighted to be doing this work and invite your prayers and support.